TRUE
Authority

Colin Urquhart

Kingdom Faith Resources Ltd.
Roffey Place, Old Crawley Road,
HORSHAM West Sussex, RH12 4RU
Tel: 01293 851543 Fax: 01293 854610
E-mail: resources@kingdomfaith.com
www.kingdomfaith.com

First published in Great Britain in March 2003 by Kingdom Faith

Kingdom Faith Trust is a registered charity (no.278746)

Unless otherwise stated, Scripture taken from the
HOLY BIBLE, NEW INTERNATIONAL VERSION.
Copyright © 1973, 1978, 1984 by International Bible Society.
Used by permission of Hodder and Stoughton Limited.

ISBN 1-900409-40-2

Acknowledgements

It is a great privilege to know Jesus as Lord. Without Him we would have no spiritual authority, and I am so thankful to Him for all He has taught me about the security of living under His authority, and how to exercise the authority He gives us as believers.

My thanks also to Rae-Anne for gathering together the material for the book from my teaching cassettes on this subject; to Mary for her work on the Word Processor; to David and Cliss for their design work.

I am continually thankful for the encouragement I receive from my fellow elders at Kingdom Faith, Michael Barling and Les Mitchell; for my personal assistant, Paula, and all at Kingdom Faith who together outwork the principles expressed in this book.

And, of course, my gratitude to the Lord for my wife, Caroline, and to all the members of my family who have prospered by living under the authority of Jesus Christ, our Lord.

Colin Urquhart

CONTENTS

1

JESUS CHRIST IS LORD

Every true Christian affirms: "Jesus Christ is Lord." There is no doubt or question of this truth; it is the basic statement of faith for any believer. Jesus Christ is the Son of God; He is Lord; He is God.

He existed before time began, entered our world for just over thirty years as both fully God and fully man. He then returned to heaven from where He had come, and now reigns in triumph, majesty and glory as Lord of Lords and King of kings.

To say that He is Lord is to say that God is the ultimate or highest authority, both in heaven and on earth. Jesus is the Word of God by whom all creation came into being. God spoke and the Word that went forth from Him brought about the creation of the entire universe.

So Jesus is Lord over all creation; He has authority over all that exists. And He has a plan for the creation He has brought into being and will ensure that this purpose is fulfilled.

This does not mean that all know Him as Lord or acknowledge His authority. Because of man's selfish, sinful nature he has the desire to be his own master and lord. The flesh (man operating independently of God) hates the idea of submission and obedience. People naturally prefer independence – the worst sin in the Bible, because it gives birth to pride, which is at the heart of all sin.

Jesus makes it clear that no one can be born again and be part of God's Kingdom unless he or she repents and believes in Him as Lord. To repent includes, not only turning away from a life of sin, but turning to God, submitting the heart to God's authority. The Christian invites Jesus to be not only his or her Saviour, but also his or her Lord. By calling Him 'Lord,' the believer is saying he or she is willing to submit to Jesus' supreme authority.

JESUS CHRIST IS TO RULE OVER THE BELIEVER, IN AND THROUGH HIM OR HER.

Jesus Christ is to rule *over* **the believer**, *in* **and** *through* **him or her.** By submitting to His authority, it will be possible to see His authority expressed in his or her life.

The possibilities that this opens up for us are limitless. Jesus said: *"Everything is possible for him who believes." (Mark 9: 23)* He said that He had not found anyone to match the faith of a Roman Centurion because the Roman soldier understood the principle of authority. Everyone, even His opponents, recognised that Jesus was a man of authority, and questioned Him as to the source of this authority. *"Where does this authority come from?"* they asked. So the Centurion was not unique in seeing that Jesus expressed great authority.

The crowds recognised that Jesus taught with authority, and witnessed His miracles that were often the result of speaking a word of release with authority, to the person who was bound in some way. *"Be opened,"* and the blind eyes were opened, death ears and dumb mouths were opened. *"Get up and walk;"* the lame and paralysed man was healed. *"Peace, be still,"* and the disciples saw the storm cease. *"Lazarus, come out,"* and the dead man was restored to life. What authority! And what power resulted from this authority!

IMAGINE WHAT POWER WE COULD SEE IN OUR LIVES, AND EXPERIENCE AS CHRISTIANS, IF WE EXPRESSED SUCH FAITH!

However, it was the centurion who realised that only someone under a higher authority could exercise such authority. Nobody else seemed to have come to the obvious conclusion that such things would not be possible unless authority and power to do them was given by God Himself. So although Jesus offered to come to the centurion's house to heal his sick servant, the soldier said this would not be necessary: "But just say the word, and my servant will be healed." (Matthew 8: 8) Just give the command, Jesus; that will be enough!

Imagine what power we could see in our lives, and experience as Christians, if we expressed such faith! "Lord, you only have to speak, to give the command." Imagine how much more effective believers would be when they prayed, how much more expectant! Think how every born again person would have a completely different understanding of the Bible. Instead of seeing this as a book of comfort and instruction, they would perceive these as the very words of God Himself; words to be believed and obeyed, rather than analysed, discussed and simply studied out of interest.

Again and again Jesus encouraged people to believe what He said, and gave them wonderful promises concerning the fruit of such faith. He went further by teaching clearly that such authority was to be expressed by the disciples both in their ministries and when they prayed:

> *I tell you the truth: if anyone says to this mountain,*
> *'Go, throw yourself into the sea,' and does not doubt in his heart*
> *but believes that what he says will happen, it will be done*
> *for him. (Mark 11:23)*

As a believer, this is the faith and authority God wants to see expressed in your life. How is this possible? How can you come to such a place in your relationship with Jesus Christ whereby you know you can speak, act and pray with authority – like your Master and Lord?

2

CREATED TO RULE

God created man in His own image and commanded him to rule over the rest of creation:

> *God blessed them and said to them, "Be fruitful and increase in number; fill the earth and subdue it. Rule over the fish of the sea and the birds of the air and over every living creature that moves on the ground." (Genesis 1: 28)*

So man was created to have authority, and while he walked in fellowship with God in the garden paradise, he was able to exercise that authority.

Once the devil had deceived Eve, and Adam had chosen to sin by disobeying the command God had given him not to eat of the tree in the middle of the garden, the whole situation changed. "The Lord God banished him from the Garden of Eden." Having rebelled against the authority of God, Adam and Eve were no longer able to exercise the same authority as before.

Because God had created man to rule, He wanted to restore his ability to do so. First, he would have to be brought back to obedient submission to God's authority; only then would he be able to exercise authority – and in a greater way than before. **Not only would he have authority over creation; he would also be able to exercise authority over all the works of the devil who had tempted and deceived him.**

Throughout the Old Testament we see the continued failure of God's people to obey His commands. When they were obedient He caused them to prosper. Then they would become complacent and disobedient. It had become their nature to sin against God by pleasing themselves instead of submitting to Him. Even though He kept faith with them, they refused to remain faithful to Him!

> NOT ONLY WOULD HE HAVE AUTHORITY OVER CREATION; HE WOULD ALSO BE ABLE TO EXERCISE AUTHORITY OVER ALL THE WORKS OF THE DEVIL WHO HAD TEMPTED AND DECEIVED HIM.

This not only deprived the nation of the authority and power God wanted His people to have over their enemies; it deprived them also of all the blessings through which the Lord wanted to cause His people to prosper.

Submission to the authority of God, and obedience to His commands that was the outworking of this submission, would enable the people to lay hold of the wonderful inheritance promised them by God. Their rebellion and disobedience demonstrated their lack of love for God. Instead of living in fear and awe of His great majesty and power, they closed their hearts against His will and only frustrated His purposes.

The law that God gave His people was good; but because of the corruption of their hearts, they were unable to keep it! Their sin continued to keep them separate from God, alienated from close fellowship and relationship with Him.

A new covenant relationship with Him would be needed. He would give His people new hearts and put His Spirit within them and empower them to obey. He would actually come to live in them, enabling them to do His will; although they would still have to choose that will over and above their own desires.

However, before this new relationship could be established it would be necessary for His holy and just judgment on sin to be executed. Disobedience had brought about spiritual death and eternal separation from God. Only a perfectly obedient life, completely submitted to God's authority could undo the work of that disobedience.

3

THE MISSION OF JESUS

To undo the sin of Adam, God had to send His Son to do these things:

To live the obedient life Adam had failed to live, and be totally submitted to God's authority and will. Although sinless Himself, to take all the sin and failure of the people upon Himself, and suffer on their behalf the death penalty they deserved.

To impart to them God's gift of eternal life, that they might live in fellowship with Him here on earth, fulfilling His will in the power of the Holy Spirit, and then be raised to live and reign with Him in the glory of heaven.

The fact that Jesus, the Word that had come from God's mouth to speak all creation into being, should leave heaven's glory and come to share our humanity, is wonder enough. The fact that He came as the Suffering Servant to give His life for sinners, is even more amazing.

Before He could make His death on the cross the sacrifice that was needed to restore us to God, He had to be identified with us

JESUS HAD TO REMAIN PERFECT. THIS ENTAILED PERFECT SUBMISSION TO THE AUTHORITY OF HIS FATHER.

completely. He needed to share our weakness and be tempted in every way that we are, yet without ever falling into sin. His obedience had to be real, succeeding where every other person had failed.

At the very beginning of His ministry, Jesus came to the River Jordan to be baptised by John the Baptist. Again this was an act of complete identification with our need. After coming out of the water, the Holy Spirit came on Jesus and God's voice from heaven said:

This is my Son, whom I love; with him
I am well pleased. (Matthew 3: 17)

Why should the Father be pleased with Jesus when His ministry had not even begun? Because for about thirty years Jesus had obediently waited for the Father's timing. During that time He did not preach or teach, neither did He heal anyone, deliver people from demonic powers or perform other miracles, including raising the dead. Everything had to be done exactly as His Father wanted and in His Father's timing. It would only take one act of disobedience or independence to repeat Adam's sin; then there would be no salvation for anyone.

Jesus had to remain perfect. This entailed perfect submission to the authority of His Father.

As soon as the Holy Spirit came on Him, He was lead into the wilderness where He fasted for forty days while being tempted by the devil. Satan wanted Jesus to use the anointing He had received for Himself, rather than in obedience to the Father; but Jesus resisted him at every point:

Man does not live on bread alone, but on every word that proceeds from the mouth of God. (Matthew 4: 4)

It is also written: 'Do not put the Lord your God to the test.' (Matthew 4: 7)

Worship the Lord your God, and serve him only. (Matthew 4:10)

Each answer demonstrated that Jesus had not come for His own purposes; He was sent by the Father to do His will. Jesus teaches this clearly again and again making several statements that demonstrate He had to live at one with His Father, perfectly obedient to His authority and will.

I tell you the truth, the Son can do nothing by himself; he can do only what he sees his Father doing, because whatever the Father does the Son also does. (John 5: 19)

It is amazing that Jesus, the Son of God, should say that He could do nothing by Himself, especially when we see the obvious authority He exercised during His ministry. **He wanted His disciples to understand that He could only exercise such authority because He remained submitted to His Father's will.**

HE COULD ONLY EXERCISE SUCH AUTHORITY BECAUSE HE REMAINED SUBMITTED TO HIS FATHER'S WILL.

For I have come down from heaven not to do my will but to do the
will of him who sent me. (John 6: 38)

Even though He is the Word of God, Jesus says:

I do nothing on my own but speak just what the Father
has taught me. (John 8:28)

Jesus said He had come to honour the Father. The miracles He performed were the result of the Father working through the Son. He even said:

Do not believe me unless I do
what my Father does. (John 10: 37)

Jesus demonstrated that He and the Father were one; there was perfect unity between them. And yet, at the same time, because of the limitations of His humanity, He could say that the Father was greater than He.

The world must learn that I love the Father
and that I do exactly what my Father
has commanded me. (John 14: 31)

This obedience was imperative if Jesus was to remain in His Father's love. Disobedience at any point would destroy the very reason for His being sent to earth as the Lamb of God that would be sacrificed to take away the sin of the world.

If you obey my commands, you will remain in my love,
just as I have obeyed my Father's commands and
remain in his love. (John 15: 10)

Here Jesus makes it clear that just as it was necessary for Him to obey His Father, so it is essential for His disciples to emulate Him by obeying His commands. If they submitted to the authority of Jesus they would not only remain in His love, but His power could be expressed through them in wonderful ways

> *I tell you the truth, anyone who has faith in me*
> *will do what I have been doing. He will do even greater*
> *things than these, because I am going to the Father.*
> *And I will do whatever you ask in my name.*
> *(John 14: 12-13)*

Such wonderful promises are the effect of submission of authority: Jesus' submission to His Father's authority, our submission to Jesus' authority.

Jesus' reward would be a return to the glory of heaven. He prayed:

> *I have brought you glory on earth by completing the work*
> *you gave me to do. And now, Father, glorify me*
> *in your presence with the glory I had with you*
> *before the world began. (John 17: 4-5)*

You only have to look at the authority Jesus exercised during His ministry to understand the wisdom and fruitfulness that results from submission to God's authority. He made it plain that by His submission to His Father, the authority and power of His Father could be expressed in all He said and did. Even so with us. **The more we are submitted to Jesus, the more of His authority can be expressed in what we say and do in His name.**

4

THE ULTIMATE ACT OF SUBMISSION

Jesus was a man of authority because He was under His Father's authority!

> *During the days of Jesus' life on earth, he offered up prayers and petitions with loud cries and tears to the one who could save him from death, and he was heard because of his reverent submission. Although he was a son, he learned obedience from what he suffered and, once made perfect, he became the source of eternal salvation for all who obey him.*
> *(Hebrews 5: 7-9)*

This does not mean Jesus was imperfect and had to be made perfect! The word means 'to be complete.' Through completing obediently the suffering He came to undertake for us, He became the source of our eternal salvation! Jesus prayed:

> *My Father, if it is possible, may this cup be taken from me. Yet not as I will, but as you will. (Matthew 26: 39)*

THE SACRIFICIAL LAMB OF GOD THAT GAVE HIS LIFE ON THE CROSS, IS NOW THE LAMB IS THE MIDST OF THE THRONE OF HEAVEN, REIGNING ETERNALLY.

Jesus knew that on the cross He would have to bear the full impact of God's wrath and experience being completely forsaken by Him! This was a terrible prospect. But His submission to His Father's authority and will meant that we could be spared from the wrath we deserve because of our sin. It was our punishment that He took upon Himself, a punishment He never deserved because He was without sin! Yet He was prepared to undertake this suffering because of His obedience to the Father, His love for us and because of the joy that was set before Him:

After he had provided purification for sins, he sat down at the right hand of the Majesty in heaven. So he became as much superior to the angels as the name he has inherited is superior to theirs. (Hebrews 1: 3-4)

While on earth, angels ministered to Jesus, especially in times of extreme stress, during the temptations in the wilderness and while experiencing the time of agony in the Garden of Gethsemane prior to His arrest. Now, having been raised triumphantly from the grave and restored to heaven, He again assumes His right to reign over the heavenly host as well as over all on the earth.

The sacrificial Lamb of God that gave His life on the cross, is now the Lamb is the midst of the throne of heaven, reigning eternally. Through His mercy and grace we, too, who believe in Him shall reign with Him.

First we are to do what He did: live in reverent submission while on earth to the authority of our heavenly Father and His Son, Jesus. He has given us the power of His own Spirit to enable us to do this.

This is the same Spirit that indwelt Jesus during His life of obedience on earth; the same Spirit that took Him through the times of temptation, enabled His submission to His Father's will in going to the cross; that raised Him from the dead, and was sent from heaven when He returned to be with the Father. **This is *His* Spirit; the Spirit of God Himself living in you. The obedient, yet all powerful Spirit of God. The Spirit that gives authority and releases God's power into our lives.**

This is the same Spirit Jesus needed throughout His ministry on earth, and is now living in you as a born again believer. Jesus says of the Spirit:

ANYTHING GOD SAYS TO US AS FATHER, SON AND HOLY SPIRIT, HAS HIS FULL AUTHORITY AND IS TO BE BELIEVED AND OBEYED.

But the Counselor, the Holy Spirit, whom the Father will send in my name, will teach you all things and will remind you of everything I have said to you. (John 14: 26)

Why does the Holy Spirit do this? We are not to ignore God's words to us, nor disbelieve Him, nor disobey Him. **Anything God says to us as Father, Son and Holy Spirit, has His full authority and is to be believed and obeyed.** Then we shall see the promises contained in His Word fulfilled in our lives.

All that belongs to the Father is mine. That is why I said
the Spirit will take from what is mine and
make it known to you. (John 16: 15)

Here is an amazing statement, for Jesus is saying that **everything the Father and the Son has, the Holy Spirit wants to convey to us.** God wants us to live in the fullness of His life that Jesus came to impart. So much is available to us for He, *"has blessed us in the heavenly realms with every spiritual blessing in Christ." (Eph 1: 3)*

Everything that is in Christ is ours, just as in the days of His humanity, everything that belonged to the Father was available to Jesus. He lived in obedient submission to the will of His Father, and so was able to avail Himself of these riches.

With such a rich inheritance available to us we have every incentive to submit to God's authority, to recognise that Jesus is rightfully the Lord of every part and aspect of our lives.

5

SO WHAT'S THE PROBLEM?

If God has given us such a rich inheritance to enjoy now, why do so many Christians show little evidence of those riches? Why, if such authority is available, do so many believers seem to exercise so little of it? Why is the Church often ridiculed instead of seen to be the people of authority and power God intends them to be? After all, everyone, even His opponents, recognised Jesus' authority, although they did not want to submit to Him!

Certain things are obvious. Jesus had great authority when He taught; yet He spoke only the words given Him by His Father. Clearly, Jesus had to believe the revelation He was receiving in order to then speak it. If we disagree with the revelation of scripture, the words God has given us, we deprive ourselves of authority. For there is no authority in our own ideas and opinions! The authority of God is in His words, not ours! So we are urged:

> *Trust in the Lord with all your heart and lean not on your own understanding; in all your ways acknowledge him, and he will make your paths straight. Do not be wise in your own eyes. (Proverbs 3: 5-7)*

Clearly, then, unbelief concerning God's Word will undermine the authority we would otherwise have when believing the Word and speaking it boldly in His name. God's authority is in what He has said. **When we agree with what He says, that authority is released into our lives; when our words are in complete agreement with His words we can express His authority. We can preach with authority, command sickness to leave with authority, cast out demons with authority and even raise the dead when God gives us the authority to do so!**

When we exalt our own thinking above the thoughts of God, we are clearly guilty of pride in imagining that we know better than the One who created the universe. That pride has serious consequences, for it leads to rebellion against God's authority, which is really what is expressed when we choose to contradict what He says. Those who rebel against His authority cannot manifest His authority! Consequently, they make themselves vulnerable to the enemy, who is the chief rebel. James reminds us that Scripture says:

God opposes the proud but gives grace to the humble. (James 4: 6)

He reminds his readers that if they are going to be successful in resisting the attacks of the enemy, they need first to submit themselves to the authority of God!

Submit yourselves, then, to God. Resist the devil
and he will flee from you. (James 4: 7)

Many try to resist the devil without submission to God, and then wonder why their exercise of 'authority' seems ineffective. The devil is not afraid of the proud hearted that do not submit themselves to God and the authority of His Word. **When a believer is in heart submission to Jesus, the devil them comes up against the One to whom that believer is submitted! And he is afraid of Jesus and flees!** Try to resist him on your own without submitting yourself to the Lord and you will suffer many disappointments!

Jesus gave authority to His disciples, "to overcome all the power of the enemy; nothing will harm you." (Luke 10: 19) So any disciple has authority. But it is the exercise of that authority we are concerned about. It is only by being in heart submission to God that we are able to exercise effectively the authority entrusted to us by Jesus! This authority is certainly for all believers, for immediately after this Jesus prayed:

> *I praise you Father, Lord of heaven and earth, because*
> *you have hidden these things from the wise and learned, and*
> *revealed them to little children. Yes, Father, for this*
> *was your good pleasure. (Luke 10: 21)*

The seventy-two that Jesus had sent out had just returned elated that even the demonic spirits submitted when they confronted them with authority in Jesus' name. He tells them not to rejoice that the demons submit, but that their names are written in heaven.

In other words, Jesus tells them to rejoice in why the demons submit to them. Believers have the authority of heaven available to them because they are God's children. By contrast, the devil and his fallen angels were thrown out of heaven. So the disciples have a greater authority than any powers that submit to the devil rather than to God.

This is true for all believers today. He that is in us (the Holy Spirit) is greater than he that is in the world (the devil)! *(see 1 John 4: 4)* Jesus gives extraordinary authority to those who believe in Him:

> *I tell you the truth, whatever you bind on earth will have been bound in heaven, and whatever you loose on earth will have been loosed in heaven. (Matthew 18: 18, literal translation)*

Jesus does not mean that when we bind something on earth it is then bound in heaven. No, the reverse! Whatever heaven binds or prevents, we have the authority to bind or prevent on earth. Whatever heaven looses or releases, we have the authority to release on earth. Jesus does not mention demonic powers specifically; He says this is true of "whatever" we bind or loose. This would include authority over the powers of darkness, but clearly includes much more, including the authority to release the good things with which God wants to bless His people.

When we understand that we prevent or release on earth what is prevented or released in heaven, then we see clearly the need to be submitted to God's authority in heaven. When we take matters into our own hands we are destined to fail. **When we submit to His authority, to His will, to His Word, to His Lordship, to the truth of the Holy Spirit, then the authority of heaven itself is expressed in what we say and do.**

This is not complicated, it is simply the consequence of what is happening in the heart of the believer. A submitted heart will enable any believer to express considerable authority in his or her life!

6

A SUBMITTED HEART

God looks, not on the outward appearance, but on the heart! He can see whether there is true heart submission or whether we are trying to appear obedient in what we do, while hiding a bitter, resentful or even rebellious heart attitude. He is concerned, not only with what we do, but the motive with which we do it.

It is very difficult to know our own hearts! For example, there are some who believe they really love the Lord and are submitted to Him, but they live very independent lives with little interaction with others. The Word of God teaches us that if we do not love those we do see, we cannot love God, who we do not see. The one who says he loves God, but does not love his or her brother or sister is self-deceived.

There are others who spend much time reading and studying the Scriptures but are very short on action, on putting the word into operation. Again we are instructed:

> *Do not merely listen to the word, and so deceive yourselves.*
> *Do what it says. (James 1: 22)*

These categories of people may be very sincere, but are self-deceived. In such cases, there will be little authority expressed in their lives. **For authority does not come from hearing the Word but from submitting to God by doing what He says.**

It is clear that the proud, independent heart attitudes need to be addressed if we are to be men and women of authority! Jesus, the man of great authority and power said that He had a gentle, humble heart. In other words, a submitted heart, is both gentle and humble.

During his early days as one of Jesus' disciples, Peter did not find submission easy. Several years later he wrote:

> *All of you, clothe yourselves with humility toward one another,*
> *because, "God opposes the proud but gives grace to the humble."*
> *Humble yourselves, therefore, under God's mighty hand, that he may*
> *lift you up in due time. (1 Peter 5: 5-6)*

Peter had learned his lesson the hard way! It was Peter who proclaimed Jesus as the Messiah and was congratulated by Jesus for receiving this revelation from the Father. However, now they know for certain who He is, Jesus chooses this occasion to warn them of His coming rejection, crucifixion and resurrection. This does not fit in with Peter's ideas of Messiahship. So he takes Jesus aside and says to Him: *"Never, Lord! This shall never happen to you!"* *(Matthew 16: 22)*

> *Jesus turned and said to Peter, "Get behind me, Satan!*
> *You are a stumbling block to me; you do not have in mind the*
> *things of God, but the things of men." (Matthew 16: 23)*

One moment Peter is the mouthpiece for God, the next for Satan. How come? One moment he is submitting to the revelation he is given, the next he is arguing with Jesus! Having just recognised Him as God's Son he then chooses to disagree with Him!

While we argue with God we are hardly in a position to exercise authority in His name!

The lesson was not easily learned. When Jesus warned His disciples that they would all desert Him in His hour of need, Peter affirmed: *"Even if all fall away on account of you, I never will."* (Matthew 26: 33) Brave words, no doubt sincerely meant. However, Jesus warns that before dawn Peter will have denied him three times. To his shame, Jesus words proved correct – as always!

Jesus did not condemn Peter, but restored him. In due course Peter got the message! Otherwise he would not have been able to write what he did about submission. Note, however, that he talked of submitting to one another. That, surely, is even more difficult than submitting to the Lord's authority! No, it is one and the same.

The one with a submitted heart will submit to the Lord's authority, wherever He chooses to place His authority.

Of course we are all to submit to Him directly as the Lord and Master of our lives. **To say that Jesus is Lord is to say He is the supreme authority. To say that He is your Lord is to say that He is the supreme authority in your life! He is the one who has every right to tell you what to do and expect obedience.** He can direct the course of your life and demand that you fulfill the plan and purpose He has for you. He desires your submission to come out of genuine love for Him, rather than the fears of the negative consequences that can result from disobedience. He is the Lord who loves you; and He wants you to be the child who loves Him!

Jesus expects you to submit to the authority of His Word, for you cannot separate His authority from the authority with which He speaks and addresses His people! To believe His words is to act on them – true submission to the authority of His Word is expressed in active faith that produces the works of faith.

JESUS EXPECTS YOU TO SUBMIT TO THE AUTHORITY OF HIS WORD

So far, so good! We should not have any problems with the principle of submitting to the authority of God and of His Son Jesus. Nor to the idea of submitting to the authority of His Word, for God is perfect and His words are the perfect revelation of His mind and will.

From this point on, though, we have greater challenges to our proud hearts! The idea of submitting to the authority of the Holy Spirit should be just as obvious. Just as God and the revelation of God's Word is perfect, so is the Holy Spirit, who is the third person in the Trinity of God. **To submit to the Spirit is to submit to God.**

However, we have to hear and receive the revelation of the Holy Spirit through imperfect channels, either by hearing Him for ourselves or through others. Paul warns that our prophecy, hearing God's voice by the Spirit, is imperfect. How are we to submit to the imperfect revelation that others may have received, or that we have heard for ourselves?

God's word challenges us still further, for God has chosen to give authority to imperfect men and women, some of whom may not even be Christians.

> *Remind the people to be subject to rulers and authorities,*
> *to be obedient, to be ready to do whatever may be good,*
> *to slander no one, to be peaceable and considerate, and*
> *to show true humility to all men. (Titus 3: 1-2)*

Can God really expect us to submit to His authority placed even in secular institutions of government? Certainly!

> *Everyone must submit himself to the governing authorities, for*
> *there is no authority except that which God has established. The*
> *authorities that exist have been established by God. Consequently, he*
> *who rebels against the authority is rebelling against what God has*
> *instituted, and those who do so will bring judgment on themselves.*
> *(Romans 13: 1-2)*

Before obeying such scriptures we want to check on the righteousness and integrity of the government. However such an attitude misses the point. The Bible sees God's sovereignty overarching the destiny of nations. He has the ability to raise up and pull down. Even the destiny of nations is in His hands. Of course, He wants to deliver people from oppressive, ungodly regimes, even though He allows such to exist. He delivered the nation of Israel from the oppressive dictatorship in Egypt. Such ungodly powers exist because the whole world is under the power of the evil one. However the only alternative to government, even when corrupt, is anarchy; that would have even more devastating consequences!

It is submission to His authority that concerns the Lord, so that we can live in His order and be churches of His authority and power. We will only affect worldly attitudes for good if we are submitted to the One who has power, even over those authorities. Remember, Jesus taught us to pray that His Kingdom will come and His will be done on earth as in heaven. In other words, He wants His heavenly rule to be established on earth. It is for the Church to demonstrate that rule and what it means to submit to His government.

God is a God of order. In every institution there has to be order, with different levels of authority; those in authority and those under authority. Without such order there would be anarchy. There has to be authority and order in a school or college, in a business or factory, in the armed forces and in civic institutions. And God has His order for the family:

> *Wives, submit to your husbands as is fitting in the Lord.*
> *Husbands, love your wives and do not be harsh with them.*
> *Children obey your parents in everything, for this*
> *pleases the Lord. (Colossians 3: 18-20)*

Behind all these instructions is God's concern for the welfare of His people. The wife's submission is to be a response to her husband's love. He is not to be harsh or controlling! When things are in God's order, people prosper. But when they are out of order this gives opportunity for negative things to afflict God's people, and the enemy is quick to seize such opportunities. Even slaves are to be submissive to their masters:

> *Slaves, obey your earthly masters in everything; and do it,*
> *not only when their eye is on you and to win their favour,*

but with sincerity of heart and reverence for the Lord.
(Colossians 3: 22)

However masters are encouraged to deal well with their slaves, because, *"you also have a Master in heaven." (Colossians 4: 1)*

Do not threaten them, since you know that he who is both
their Master and yours is in heaven, and there is no favouritism
with him. (Ephesians 6: 9)

It is, therefore, a great responsibility to have authority, for God is going to hold people accountable for the ways in which they have exercised that authority. God does not expect people to abuse their use of authority, to oppress, manipulate or use their position to serve their own ends.

To be given authority by God is to serve His ends and purposes. He expects those in authority to be concerned about the welfare of those under their authority. Nowhere should this be more evident than in God's Church.

However, it is important for us to understand that Christians are called upon to be good citizens as part of their witness.

Therefore, it is necessary to submit to the authorities,
not only because of possible punishment but also because of
conscience. This is also why you pay taxes, for the authorities
are God's servants, who give their full time to governing.
Give everyone what you owe him: If you owe taxes, pay taxes;
if revenue, then revenue; if respect, then respect; if honour,
then honour. (Romans 13: 5-7)

It is easy to be critical of government and other authorities instead of praying for them! Those who have never experienced the complications of being in government can be quick to criticise what is wrong, but are often slow to praise what is right! Such is human nature!

7
AUTHORITY IN THE CHURCH

Christians have to learn both how to be in authority and under authority. In the church there is to be another standard of government from that which is possible in the world. Jesus says:

You know that the rulers of the Gentiles lord it over them, and their high officials exercise authority over them. Not so with you. Instead, whoever wants to be great among you must be your servant, and whoever wants to be first must be your slave - just as the Son of Man did not come to be served, but to serve, and to give his life as a ransom for many. (Matthew 20: 25-28)

In God's Kingdom there is certainly an order of authority; but it's standards are almost the opposite of those of the world! Men who live according to the flesh, their natural desires, want prestige, position and power because of the control it gives them over others for their own selfish purposes. Such things must never be in God's Church. The exercise of authority is never to be controlling or manipulating.

Jesus was the man of greatest authority ever to walk on the face of the earth. He neither controlled or manipulated, for He is love.

TO BE GREAT IN THE EYES OF GOD IS TO BE TRULY HUMBLE, TO BE WILLING TO LOVE, CARE FOR AND SERVE THOSE OVER WHOM YOU EXERCISE AUTHORITY.

Those who control and manipulate do not love those they lead and over whom they are to exercise spiritual authority.

Jesus had a humble, gentle heart; yet clearly exercised great authority. He was the most authoritive because He was the most submitted to the authority of the Father! He was the greatest *servant.* **To be great in the eyes of God is to be truly humble, to be willing to love, care for and serve those over whom you exercise authority.** It is unthinkable that a Christian leader would use a position of authority for his own ends, or advancement. In serving the people he is serving Christ! Whatever he does to them, he does to the Lord! On the Day of Judgment the Lord will hold him accountable for the way in which he has used the authority given him.

We can at once see that all too often, where true spiritual authority is lacking in church leadership, there is instead an authoritarian approach. This is man's fleshly, and therefore sinful, substitute for genuine spiritual authority.

Authoritarianism is an assumed rather than a given authority! God raises up the humble. The proud raise themselves up and assume positions of authority and responsibility never given them by God. This is when you see clear evidence of control and manipulation. Instead of teaching people to be responsible disciples, much of their personal decision - making is taken away from them under such leadership. They are told what to do, and unless they obey, are accused of being rebellious!

It is clear that the leading ministries in the Church are to be enabling ministries. They are not to crush people but build them up. They are to, *"prepare God's people for works of service, so that the body of Christ may be built up." (Ephesians 4: 12)* Leaders are to build up, not suppress. They are to encourage and enable, not make people passive in their attitudes. **The leaders are to be there for the people, then the people will be there for the leaders!**

Leadership is to be by example; showing people what to do, rather than simply telling them what to do!

> *Remember your leaders, who spoke the word of God to you.*
> *Consider the outcome of their way of life and imitate*
> *their faith. (Hebrews 13: 7)*

The authority of the Word of God is to be supreme. So the responsible leader is one who speaks this Word to the people, keeping the direction of their personal lives and corporate life in line with the truth, as revealed in scripture. The leader will demonstrate the outworking of this teaching in his or her life-style, and will give an example of how to live by faith. The leader is to have a faith that can be imitated.

DEPENDENCE ON GOD'S WORD, A RIGHTEOUS LIFE-STYLE AND A WALK OF FAITH WHAT A POWERFUL COMBINATION!

Dependence on God's Word, a righteous life-style and a walk of faith - what a powerful combination! True authority will be evidenced by a leader who lives in this way. It is important that, although no leader is perfect, the people have confidence in his leadership because they perceive him to be a person of integrity. When he does make a mistake, he is big enough to acknowledge this openly, rather than try to justify his error in any way. To do that would very quickly lend to an erosion of authority in his leadership. Those who govern well are to be given double honour. They are doubly accountable to the Lord, for their own personal walk with Him, and also for the way in which they have led others; and so they are worthy of being given double honour.

8

SUBMISSION TO AUTHORITY

Position does not give a person spiritual authority. This comes from a leader's submission to the Lord. He can only exercise as much authority as he is himself submitted to the Lord's authority. The wisdom of the Holy Spirit is evident in the way a submitted man or women leads and makes decisions.

This is not the place for a detailed discussion of the various structures of church leadership that exist. Some are biblically based; others are not! Certainly the desire for office because a person wants prestige, recognition or control is totally wrong, as we have seen. Church members are urged to give double honour to *"the elders who direct the affairs of the church well."* (1 Timothy 5: 17) They are not honoured simply because they are elders, but because they govern *well.*

Paul gives a comprehensive list of the qualities that are to be evidenced in the life-style demonstrated by elders. Such people will certainly be worthy of respect and honour; and therefore their authority will be recognised readily by most. Of course, any proud or rebellious hearts are always slow to respond to authority, no matter how godly.

THE LEADER IS TO COMMAND RESPECT BECAUSE HE PROVES WORTHY OF IT.

The general principle is that if those in leadership cannot exercise proper authority and leadership in his family life, then they will not be able to "take care of God's church." (see 1 Timothy 3: 2-5) This is further indication that leadership is by example not control.

The leader is to command respect because he proves worthy of it. Those under his authority recognise that it is God who has raised up such leaders. They are a gift to the Body of Christ. In submitting to their authority, they are in effect submitting to the Lord's authority being expressed through them.

Every congregation is to be a local expression of the Body of Christ, every member working together in unity for the welfare of all the others. They need positive direction and prophetic leadership from those who have the responsibility to hear from God. This is one of the principle needs for leaders, for a congregation is not to be manipulated by so-called prophetic voices in the congregation. All prophecy is to be tested by the leadership. God can and does confirm the spiritual direction of a church by prophetic utterance. But the responsibility to hear from God is in the hands of the leaders, especially the leader of the leaders. All who preach and teach should do so in line with the prophetic direction in which God is leading His people.

Without such authoritative leadership, either a church will effectively go nowhere, or it will be pulled in different directions by different voices, a recipe for division.

Such division was a potential danger in the early church with Gentile and Jewish believers coming from diametrically opposing backgrounds. Even a spiritual heavyweight like the apostle Paul was ready to submit himself and what he was teaching to the Council of apostles and elders in Jerusalem. It was they who made the necessary decisions, which were then relayed back to the churches through Paul, Barnabas and others. The Council wrote a letter of authority to be recognised by all the churches.

We see here the concern to be held accountable to the highest authority, in the expectation that these council members would most readily be able to interpret God's mind over the matters raised.

Because of their submissive hearts, such men as Paul and Barnabas were prepared to be held accountable for what they taught and the decisions they made. They did not want to function in independence. Paul was confident that his decisions were right; submitting them to the council added to his authority against those who opposed his teaching.

> IT IS A SIGN OF INSECURITY IN A BELIEVER IF HE IS NOT PREPARED TO SUBMIT WHAT HE BELIEVES HE HEARS FROM THE LORD TO THOSE IN HIGHER AUTHORITY.

The truly spiritual leader is never unhappy about submitting what he believes, teaches and does to others who have true spiritual authority. There is only one Holy Spirit and He will give the right witness to all who are sensitive to His voice. He will not speak contradictory things about a situation to different people.

It is a sign of insecurity in a believer if he is not prepared to submit what he believes he hears from the Lord to those in higher authority. If he is truly hearing from the Lord, then the believer can be confident that the Holy Spirit will give the same witness to other sensitive believers, especially those whom God has raised up and put in positions of spiritual authority. Otherwise every man becomes his own oracle, something that incurs judgment, not blessing!

Although it is good that in recent decades the voice of prophecy has been restored to the Church, there now needs to be a true heart submission from all who claim to hear from the Lord.

Moses was clearly the man raised up by God to lead His people out of the bondage in Egypt. Aaron was his right-hand man and supported him in that whole endeavour. However, when Moses decided to marry a Cushite woman, both Miriam and Aaron felt justified in criticising Moses.

> *Miriam and Aaron began to talk against Moses*
> *because of his Cushite wife, for he had married a Cushite.*
> *"Has the Lord spoke only through Moses?" they asked.*
> *"Hasn't he also spoken through us?" And the Lord*
> *heard this. (Numbers 12: 1-2)*

Unfortunately this is a situation all too frequently repeated today. People can be very critical of those given them by the Lord to lead them. They believe their own prophetic "revelation" has just as much weight and authority as those given to their leaders. Clearly the Lord is unimpressed by such attitudes!

Why was Moses a man of such authority? He was humble, not proud like Miriam and Aaron in daring to presume they had revelation equal to that of God's appointed man!

(Now Moses was a very humble man, more humble than anyone else on the face of the earth.) (Numbers 12: 3)

It was this humility before God that gave him such authority.

By contrast "the anger of the Lord burned against" Miriam and Aaron because of their presumption. Miriam was struck with leprosy, a sign of being unclean. The impurity was in her heart, for both Aaron and she were guilty of pride and rebellion against His authority. The Lord would not have allowed Miriam to be afflicted with such a dreadful disease, unless He needed to teach her the seriousness of their sin. Moses cries out to the Lord on her behalf, such is his compassion and the Lord answered:

"Confine her outside the camp for seven days; after that she can be brought back." So Miriam was confined outside the camp for seven days, and the people did not move on till she was brought back. (Numbers 12: 14-15)

Seven days in which to come back to having a humble, submissive heart. But notice: her rebellion prevented all the people from moving on! That is the effect of having rebellion in the camp, or in the congregation. Even if it is only present in a few hearts, it is so destructive in it's consequences that it can prevent the whole congregation from moving on in the purposes of God. The wrong heart attitude was deceptive. Both Aaron and Miriam thought they were spiritual. Many today have such attitudes. "God can speak to us, not only to the leaders," they say. But He will never speak to over-rule those to whom he has given the responsibility to lead. When He gives authority, He sticks by those to whom He has given it!

It does not seem to occur to some people that if God had wanted them to lead, He has the power to place them in a position of leadership. However, He resists the proud and raises up the humble. Self-righteousness and superior attitudes are certainly not the expression of genuine humility.

The sin of Korah, Dathian and Abriam was judged even more harshly by the Lord. They "became insolent and rose up against Moses" (Numbers 16: 2), together with 250 "well-known community leaders." Because this was a considerable number of people, you may think that they had truth on their side.

> *They came as a group to oppose Moses and Aaron and*
> *said to them, "You have gone too far! The whole community*
> *is holy, every one of them, and the Lord is with them.*
> *Why then do you set yourself above the Lord's*
> *assembly? (Numbers 16: 3)*

On the face of it this seems a right spiritual perception, even more true of the Church of the New Testament than of Israel in the Old. Surely the whole community of God's people is holy? And is not the Lord with them? So what is wrong?

Neither Israel nor the Church is a democracy. God does not place His authority in "the whole assembly." The purpose of the assembly was to support Moses in his God given authority and leadership, not oppose him. The weight of numbers was totally irrelevant. In opposing Moses, they were opposing the Lord's word spoken through him and the Lord's authority given to him.

Aaron is now on the other side of the argument. Moses' reaction is again a humble one. He falls facedown before the Lord before delivering His word to Korah and his followers. He shows them that "it is against the Lord that you and all your followers have banded together." (Numbers 16: 11) All the people are in danger of coming under the Lord's judgment.

> *But Moses and Aaron fell facedown and cried out, "O God,*
> *God of the spirits of all mankind, will you be angry with the entire*
> *assembly when only one man sins?" (Number 16: 22)*

Eventually everyone else moved back from the three ring-leaders and their families:

> *Then Moses said, "This is how you will know that the LORD*
> *has sent me to do all these things and that it was not*
> *my idea." (Numbers 16: 28)*

Moses knows that the Lord will stand by His own authority delegated to him. God's judgment was for the earth to open and swallow up the rebellious families. And fire consumed the others who had opposed Moses and Aaron. Radical measures indeed!

Rebellion in the head of a household can have serious repercussions on the whole family! Again we see God's judgment on such rebellion.

THE LORD RAISES UP THOSE WHO ARE SO SUBMITTED TO HIM, THAT THEY CHOOSE TO PLEASE HIM, RATHER THAN THEMSELVES OR OTHERS.

God does not act in such dramatic ways today under the terms of the New Covenant. However, unfortunately there are many whose spiritual lives have either deteriorated seriously, or worse has happened, because they dared to challenge the Lord's authority in those to whom he had given it. God takes such challenges against His authority very seriously!

All that has been said makes it plain that God does not raise up proud leaders, but those who have humble hearts and who are in true submission to Him. **They want to serve the people by leading them obediently in the way chosen by God.** Yet, at the same time, they are resolute. They are not man-pleasers and refuse to be drawn away from God's purposes. Paul says:

*If I were still trying to please men, I would not be
a servant of Christ (Galatians 1: 10)*

The Lord raises up those who are so submitted to Him, that they choose to please Him, rather than themselves or others.

There are many who want their own say in how things should be done. They are deceived into thinking their ideas and opinions ("revelations" even!) are just as good, or even better, than those of the leaders under whom God has placed them! Such is the deceptive nature of rebellion.

These events from Moses' experience are written for our learning. Moses was a man who knew the Lord and could talk with Him face to face. The people had been completely dependent on His leadership in times of difficulty. Yet this still did not prevent them from rising up in rebellion.

Why do so many Christians find submission to authority difficult? Obviously this is often the result of their own pride and their rebellious, independent spirits. However, there are surely occasions when leaders are wrong, for they are fallible human beings. Isn't it only reasonable, then, to criticise, correct, even oppose them when this is the case?

Not if we are talking about true spiritual leadership, appointed by God. Of course if an individual Christian finds himself under false leadership he is not in the Lord's appointed place, for He does not want any of His children led by false shepherds. The *"hireling,"* Jesus says, *"cares nothing for the sheep." (John 10: 13)* He is a paid functionary and is concerned only to safeguard his position or to seek his own advancement in the structure of which he is a part.

However, it is today just as awesome a mistake to challenge true authority where God has placed it. Those under wrong authority should rapidly place themselves under true spiritual authority. For a congregation can never advance spiritually beyond its leadership. Those under the wrong leadership simply will not grow and develop in the way God intends.

Those under the right kind of spiritual authority will have to learn to submit to the Lord's authority in that situation. They will be encouraged to do so, not only because they will be taught correctly, but because they will be given a good example to follow by those leaders. They will see in them the humility, submission and servant

IT IS AN AWESOME RESPONSIBILITY TO BE IN SPIRITUAL AUTHORITY. IT IS ALSO AN AWESOME RESPONSIBILITY TO BE SUBMITTED RIGHTLY TO THAT AUTHORITY!

heart that reflects something of Jesus' attitude to His Father's authority, or Moses' humility before God.

The devil is the arch-rebel. **To challenge the authority of God in those in whom He has placed that authority, is to do the devil's work for Him!** That is not clever! Every spirit that is rebellious, proud, independent, insubmissive is serving the enemy, not God. Those with such attitudes will not be able to exercise authority over the enemy: they are not truly submitted to God, but unwittingly are joining with the enemy in opposing His authority.

It is an awesome responsibility to be in spiritual authority. It is also an awesome responsibility to be submitted rightly to that authority! Rebellious, independent attitudes can spread rapidly, and often those with such hearts are outspoken and want to influence those around them. We are to:

Submit to one another out of reverence for Christ.
(Ephesians 5: 21)

Where true submission is lacking there is not that proper reverence for Christ!

9
AUTHORITY AND ACCOUNTABILITY

It is all a matter of the heart. When the heart is proud or independent, then people do not want to be held accountable for what they believe, say or do! They are not truly surrendered to the Lord's will.

Nobody finds submission difficult when God is asking them to do things they want to do, whether directly or through the leadership. It is when there is a clash of wills that problems arise. It is then that people do not want to recognise God's authority in the leadership. If some justifiable criticism can be made of the leaders, they imagine this would excuse their disobedience to what he says.

Not so, for God knows that no one He raises up in leadership is perfect, not even Moses. But still He expects His authority to be recognised in those leaders.

Many Christians hide behind super-spiritual unrealistic phrases. What would happen to a soldier if when given an order by an officer, he said: "I will pray about it, sir," or "I don't think you have just issued the right order; please think again," or "I will only do what you say if I hear it personally from the general!"

And yet the Lord's authority is far superior to that of any army officer. Even if the officer is wrong, he is still to be obeyed. Once he has issued the order, he is responsible for the way he has exercised his authority. The soldier is safe in submission and obedience.

So it is spiritually. A willingness to obey and be held accountable is pleasing to the Lord. **If we prove faithful in being** *under* **authority, He knows it will be safe to place us** *in* **authority.**

One thing is certain, God gives all the grace needed to enable you to obey. But He will never grace you to be disobedient! To think that your spiritual life is between God and you alone is simply not true. Of course you have your personal relationship with God; but you are part of His Body and have a responsibility to move in harmony with the rest of the Body!

THE HUMBLE, SUBMITTED HEART HAS FEW PROBLEMS WITH OBEDIENCE, EVEN WHEN SUCH OBEDIENCE IS CHALLENGING.

The humble, submitted heart has few problems with obedience, even when such obedience is challenging. The fact that God has made His will about authority and submission clear in His Word is enough. The Holy Spirit will enable the necessary obedience.

To co-operate with the Spirit is life and peace. To oppose the Spirit is evidence that you are walking in the flesh and therefore in opposition to God. Jesus tells us that in our flesh there dwells nothing good! There is nothing good about opposing the Lord's will and authority! Paul prays:

I pray that out of his glorious riches he may strengthen you
with power through his Spirit in your inner being, so that Christ
may dwell in your hearts through faith.
(Ephesians 3: 16-17)

When Christ is allowed to express His life in and through us there will be submission to our heavenly Father's authority. Our walk of faith is dependent on such submission. Faith is not trying to bend God's will to your own; it is trusting God to enable you to fulfill His divine will for your life. It is being sure and certain of what we hope for and do not see! It is trusting the Lord with all your heart instead of depending on your own understanding.

When we exalt our thinking, opinions, ideas and understanding over above what God tells us to do then we find ourselves in trouble. It does not matter whether we are talking of submission to the direct authority in His Word, or delegated authority to spiritual leadership, the principle is the same. We are under the authority of the Lordship of Jesus at all times.

The only occasions when we have the right to refuse delegated authority is if we are asked to do something contradictory to God's Word. Even our refusal must be done with a submissive spirit, not with pride or arrogance. When the Jewish authorities tried to stop them preaching in the name of Jesus, Peter and the other apostles replied:

We must obey God rather than men! (Acts 5: 29)

In that situation the authorities were going against God's Word. One of their number, Gamaliel, warned that if what the apostles were doing was from God, *"you will not be able to stop these men; you will only find yourselves fighting against God."* (Acts 5:39)

You have the Lord's authority to resist anyone asking you to deny obedience to God's Word. Those who ask you to do such things, are not acting in the name of Jesus. No true spiritual authority will hinder the working and manifestation of God's Spirit; nor will they prevent the preaching of the whole counsel of God. However they will put a stop to manifestations that are not scriptural and of the Spirit, and they will correct any teaching or so-called prophetic word that is not in line with the scriptures.

Mature spiritual leadership needs to be respected, for such people have gained in wisdom, through their experience of the ways in which God works. They learn not only what to do, but how to do it. It is possible for a believer to have a correct revelation from God concerning something he is to do, but lack wisdom in how to go about putting that word obediently into action. As he submits the revelation he has received to those over him, he can receive the benefit of their wisdom and experience, and save himself from frustration and disappointment that can result from trying to do the right thing, but in the wrong way and possibly at the wrong time! Accountability is for the good of the believer!

There is not real submission without love and no real love for God without submission. Jesus said:

If you obey my commands, you will remain in my love,
just as I have obeyed my Father's commands and remain
in his love. (John 15: 10)

Our love for Jesus leads us to submit to His authority, no matter where He places that authority. Even when we don't want to submit, our love for Him will over-rule our own desires. It is important, therefore, to love those God places over us. It is not possible to moan, murmur, grumble, complain about our leaders and love them at the same time! We are to respect them and give them honour and love!

Obey your leaders and submit to their authority. They keep watch over you as men who must give an account. Obey them so that their work will be a joy, not a burden, for that would be of no advantage to you. (Hebrews 13: 17)

You are accountable to your leaders, just as they are accountable to God for you and the way in which they exercise His authority. When speaking to the elders from the church at Ephesus, Paul said:

Keep watch over yourselves and all the flock of which the Holy Spirit has made you overseers. (Acts 20:28)

It is God's Spirit who has placed them in their position of leadership, and He will enable them to fulfill their responsibilities. Paul warns them:

Savage wolves will come in among you and will not spare the flock. Even from among your own number men will arise and distort the truth in order to draw away disciples after them. (Acts 20: 29-30)

To remain under the covering or protection of true shepherds is the most secure thing for a believer to do. Such shepherds will watch out for the wolves and will have the spiritual authority to deal with them. They will not stand back and watch the wolves wreaking havoc among the sheep. Because they are men of the Word, they will be on the watch for any distortion of the truth and will be concerned to handle God's Word with love and respect when they preach and teach.

They will also be very aware of the independent, rebellious ones who will promote their opinions and ideas, often with a view to causing a split in the church by "drawing disciples after them."

OBEY AND SUBMIT

Obedience is the outward action of a submitted heart. The Lord does not want a begrudging submission from a critical heart; but a willing obedience from a loving heart.

When believers love their leaders, such submission is never a major problem, even though the faults of such leaders may be glaring at times.

OBEDIENCE IS THE OUTWARD ACTION OF A SUBMITTED HEART.

I am the leader of a major Christian work. This means I need to be the most submitted person to God's authority. I have to walk humbly before Him and others. I have to guard against any fleshly attitudes in any decisions I make. I need to spend hours sitting at Jesus' feet as I receive His Word, and listen to the voice of His Spirit. I have to be at one with those who share the ultimate authority with me for the work, not making major decisions independently but corporately with them.

I am only too aware of my own fallibility. But I have learned to acknowledge openly when I have been wrong and ask for people's forgiveness whenever this is necessary. I have to love those for whom I am responsible and be prepared to lay my life down for them in whatever ways are necessary and appropriate, if I am to expect their love for me and the honouring of God's call and anointing on my life.

If I am faithful to God's call I will inspire in those I lead confidence to walk with me in obedience to the way in which the Holy Spirit leads us as a body of believers.

GOD DOES NOT ASK HIS PEOPLE TO SUBMIT TO AN AUTHORITY HE DOES NOT RECOGNISE AND RESPECT HIMSELF.

A work can only continue to grow and expand without divisions arising if there is a right spirit in the whole Body. Such a spirit has to begin with the leadership, for whatever is in the leaders will be reproduced in those they lead.

There has to be unity around a common vision, everyone submitted to that vision. A church cannot be double sighted (or worse) and expect to be effective. If the work is to prosper, the leadership will train people, raise them up and release them in ministry; not fearful of allowing God to use others and cause their spiritual growth and development. Only the insecure leader is threatened by the way in which God uses others and causes them to prosper.

The Lord Himself respects His delegated authority in whatever sphere – government, church, business, house, family. He gives us the power to make decisions without over-ruling us, even when we make mistakes. **God does not ask His people to submit to an authority He does not recognise and respect Himself!** He puts somebody in authority and then, in a sense, submits to that authority Himself. For example, if a pastor decides to have meetings at a particular time, the Lord does not call His own meetings for another time. He respects the decision of the pastor as to when the meetings should be. He is ready to anoint the preaching of the Word and to cause His Spirit to move at those times!

Even if you have your own personal vision and revelation, God does not expect you to go against the authority He has put in place. If you have truly heard from the Lord, He will enable the outworking of that word in the right way, at the right time, in the right place. It is not for you to try to manipulate the leadership and the whole church to follow your vision, nor to implement something that would cut across the way the Lord is leading His people corporately.

A submitted heart is not a divided heart, one part desiring obedience to the Lord, the other working to promote self! We are to deny self in order to follow Jesus as true disciples.

> A SUBMITTED HEART IS NOT A DIVIDED HEART, ONE PART DESIRING OBEDIENCE TO THE LORD, THE OTHER WORKING TO PROMOTE SELF.

11

PRINCIPLES OF AUTHORITY

God has revealed many principles of authority in His Word. I will summarise these briefly as they will be useful for quick reference:

You are called to be under the Lord's authority. As soon as you are born again, Jesus is your Lord and has authority over you. Not recognising this is rebellion, which is opposition to His authority.

You are under His authority to do His will. You still have free will, but you need to submit this to Him so that He can carry out His plan for your life.

You are called to work! *"Jesus said to them, 'My Father is always at his work to this very day, and I, too, am working.'" (John 5: 17)* This is the work He wants you to fulfil as part of His Kingdom purposes.

You can do nothing by yourself; all must be done in relation and submission to God. Apart from Jesus you can do nothing!

Revelation and authority go together. God wants you to know what He is saying to you as a member of the Body of Christ, as one who desires to please Him by obeying Him. He reveals His will that you might do His will!

Avoid judging others, whether in leadership or other believers, even if you perceive that they are not in true submission to the Lord. Be sure you are submitted, and pray for those who are not!

You live to please Him, not yourself.

Do not draw attention to yourself, but to the One you serve. This is the evidence of a humble, submitted spirit.

God provides the grace you need to carry out and persevere until you finish the work He has given you to do. There is little point in saying you submit to His purpose, but then give up before that purpose has been completed.

When you speak in His name, you are to speak His words, not your own opinions. You have submitted yourself to the Truth and are willing to hold fast to that Truth with an honest and good heart!

Work for the Lord's honour and to give all the glory to Him, without seeking to glorify yourself. Jesus exercised such great authority because He wanted to glorify His Father in everything He did.

You need to be prepared to obey Him, no matter the cost, out of love for Him. Your love for Him will motivate you to do this.

You have been given authority to pray in the name of Jesus.

The Holy Spirit will guide you so that you can pray with faith, in accordance with His will.

The works you perform under His authority are His works - not yours. When He commissions you, He enables you, so all glory goes to Him!

Stay humble. He gives grace to the humble but pulls down the proud. He is your Lord in every situation.

Do exactly what He commands. Don't add to what He says or take away from the revelation He gives you.

Obedience keeps you abiding in His love. Jesus promises that the Father and Son come to make their home with those who love and obey!

You can only teach effectively what you yourself have learned from the Lord, what is living in your heart and is expressed in your life. There is no authority in the teaching of one who only speaks theoretically.

You are under the Lord's authority at all times and are accountable to Him for all you do. You cannot opt out when you feel like it and then come under His authority again when it is convenient to do so.

Everything you receive comes from the Lord and therefore is related to His will for you. Everything He does and commands is for a purpose. Therefore you can learn "to be content in all things." The Lord is in charge!

The fact that you have been given authority is a sign that God has put His seal of approval on you! He wants you to use this authority effectively and obediently.

If you honour the Lord by being submissive to Him, He will honour you. And all the rewards for obedience promised in scripture will be yours.

No matter what He gives you to do, speak and act with His authority. He is the One who has commissioned you; so He stands with you as Lord. He sends you to act in His name with all the authority at His command!

We will live in unity if we are submitted to Him as a Body of believers. It is imperative to resist all the divisive attacks of the enemy, who opposes God's authority.

Everything fruitful and effective in God in your life is the work of the Spirit within you. Do not steal the glory from Him, but be thankful to Him. Then He can lead you into greater and greater things.

You stay in the right place of submission to the authority of God through a life of prayer and worship. Humble yourself under God's mighty hand - daily!

You have all authority over the power of the evil one. When you are submitted to God the enemy has no hold over you. *"Submit yourselves, then, to God. Resist the devil and he will flee from you."* *(James 4: 7)*

The authority given to you by God is greater than any authority given by man. However you are to obey all authorities unless they go against the Word of God, and you must respect those who are over you in the Lord.

Submission means acquisition! You appropriate what belongs to you - every spiritual blessing - by living in the obedience of faith. There is no real faith without submission because submission is trusting in the Lord.

Obedience will be rewarded. *"Whoever has my commands and obeys them, he is the one who loves me. He who loves me will be loved by my Father, and I too will love him and show myself to him." (John 14: 21)* Submission to His authority will lead to a greater revelation of Jesus to you personally.

It is profitable to obey out of a heart of trust, love and humble submission to the Lord; you will prosper as a result. And He promises that His joy will be in you and that your joy will be full!

12

BENEFITS FROM BEING
UNDER AUTHORITY

To be under authority brings many benefits.

You stop fighting God. To acknowledge you are under the Lord's authority, both directly and through delegated authority, involves a surrender of your will to His will. This removes many negatives from your life and means more of His life can be expressed through you.

You no longer want to grieve Him, but want Him to have His way with you.

You have no cause to complain and grumble because you are submitted to the One who, in all things, is working for your good. Surrendering to Him brings a greater trust in Him!

You take the commands in His Word seriously. For example, you will not judge other people, for you do not want to place yourself back under judgment. You now have a bigger vision of who God is and a greater awe of His authority. You become more merciful, conscious of how merciful He is to you. He never criticises and judges you, so you in turn will be slow to judge or criticise others!

You will not take offence because of what others do to you. Offence is a failure to forgive; if you do not forgive, God will not forgive you. There is no situation in which you desire to put yourselves at odds with the Lord.

You live in the continual awareness of God's grace. Knowing you can do nothing by yourself is very liberating. You are accepted in Christ, the One who rules in supreme authority, and all His resources are available to you because of your submission to Him.

You become more like the one you are submitted to – Jesus! The greater your submission the more of His life can be reflected in you.

When God's will prevails above your own, this is victory! Before you would have considered this as a defeat, not to have your own way. Now you realise the more He has His way, the more victory you will experience.

Submission also equals protection. *"Submit yourselves, then, to God. Resist the devil and he will flee from you."* (James 4: 7)

Under His authority is also living in unity with Him. *"Jesus replied, 'If anyone loves me, he will obey my teaching. My Father will love him, and we will come to him and make our home with him.'"* (John 14: 23)

Submission leads to obedience and obedience releases many blessings into your life.

The more submitted you are, the more you are aware of the sense of His presence and the easier it is to hear His voice.

The fruit of submission is a greater fear of the Lord, filling you with a greater desire to do His will and to please Him.

You are able to enter into a new dimension of worship as you come humbly before Him, drawing closer, right into His presence.

"If a man remains in me and I in him, he will bear much fruit." (John 15: 5) You remain "in Him" by obeying His commands, and your fruitfulness brings glory to the Father. *"This is to my Father's glory, that you bear much fruit, showing yourself to be my disciples." (John 15: 8)*

You can draw near to the throne of grace with faith, with a greater awareness of God and a greater sense of His presence. Knowing you are submitted to Him gives you a greater confidence and expectancy when you pray.

Submission is key to fulfilling the ministry God gives you: to do what He wants, when He wants, in the way He wants!

By submitting and humbling yourself before Him, God can raise you up higher and higher – in worship, ministry and every way! *"All of you, clothe yourselves with humility toward one another, because, 'God opposes the proud but gives grace to the humble.' Humble yourselves, therefore, under God's mighty hand, that he may lift you up in due time." (1 Peter 5: 5-6)*

Submitting to God's authority releases His authority and power into your life. You can live victoriously over adverse circumstances as you bind what is bound in heaven, and lose what is loosed in heaven.

You become a blessing to the body of Christ because you spread a spirit of submission by your attitudes, conversation and actions. Others will learn from your example.

You become a more faithful witness of who He is, the Lord who is to be loved and obeyed at all times.

The more submitted you are, the more God can entrust to you. You prove faithful in the small things and He gives you greater responsibility, and authority!

As a leader, the more you submit to God's authority, the more you are able to lead God's people with genuine spiritual authority. This makes it easier for people to submit to the Lord's will for their lives.

Everything about God is good and positive, therefore everything that happens to you as a result of your submission to Him is good and positive. The more positives there are in your life, the less room there is for the enemy!

The more submitted to the authority of Jesus the greater your ability to exercise the authority He has given you as a believer over all the works of the enemy! You can believe His promise: *"Nothing will harm you."*

"And we know that in all things God works for the good of those who love him, who have been called according to his purpose." (Ro 8: 28)

13

LIVING IN AUTHORITY

Everything he did, Paul did out of love for Jesus and as such he spoke with a voice of authority that is evident in the epistles he wrote. He neither deserved nor wanted praise from any man. He deserved nothing, but had received everything through God's mercy and grace and, therefore, did not want to willingly go against God's purpose.

> *For I am the least of the apostles and do not even deserve to be*
> *called an apostle, because I persecuted the church of God.*
> *But by the grace of God I am what I am, and his grace to me*
> *was not without effect. No, I worked harder than all of them*
> *– yet not I, but the grace of God that was with me. Whether,*
> *then, it was I or they, this is what we preach, and this*
> *is what you believed. (1 Corinthians 15: 9-11)*

If there is no Godly authority in the Church then the body of Christ is impaired and ineffective. The Church can only be healthy when it exhibits the right authority, His authority - not just in leadership, but also in all the members.

If a leader has to appeal to his position for the exercise of authority, it is obvious that either he does not exercise true spiritual authority, or the people he leads have no respect for his authority. This is why God is careful about the way He releases authority to people. **The amount of authority given to a person depends not on his position, but on the ministry with which the Lord has entrusted him.**

The only way to respect authority is to submit to it. God will give His authority to those who respect authority, the most submitted, the most humble. However, the authority or ministry He gives never becomes yours; it always belongs to God. **What He commissions, He enables.** We serve Him allowing Him to express His life, power, ministry through us. This principle is the same for every believer, not just for those in leadership: you can only exercise authority in relation to the amount you are submitted to His authority, both directly and in those under whom He places you.

A student is not above his teacher, nor a servant above his master. It is enough for the student to be like his teacher, and the servant like his master. (Matthew 10:24-25)

God never gives His authority away; it is always His. If you are a leader you are to be responsible in exercising what belongs to Him! You are appointed to serve and represent God to those for whom you are to care.

All of you, clothe yourselves with humility toward one another, because, "God opposes the proud but gives grace to the humble." Humble yourselves, therefore, under God's mighty hand, that he may lift you up in due time. (1 Peter 5: 5-6)

Every believer has authority because he or she belongs to the Kingdom. You have the Kingdom of God within you, and can exercise His rule and reign because you are submitted yourself to His reign over you. The Lord wants you to develop a Kingdom mentality, so that you think according to the position of authority He has given you as a believer and, if appropriate, as a leader.

For example a teacher does not need to keep reminding himself that he is a teacher before dealing with a pupil. Neither does he need to tell the students that he is the teacher! Similarly we should not have to remind ourselves that we are Kingdom people; we think accordingly! Neither do we listen to any lies of the enemy suggesting we do not have authority over him and those submitted to him!

Your authority has to be expressed in what you do! You have authority to fulfil whatever commission God has given you. You have the authority to do God's will! If you are in leadership this also means bringing those God has given you under His headship, not to lord it over them but to teach them how to come under God's authority. You give an example of what it means to submit to Him.

People see that you are ready to obey God's Word and to be submitted in your heart to those who are over you. **God backs obedience to His Word with His authority and power.**

When a body of believers pray out of a position of being rightly submitted to the Lord and to one another, their prayer can be very powerful, because they will be able to pray together with authority.

I tell you the truth, anyone who has faith in me
will do what I have been doing. He will do even greater things
than these, because I am going to the Father. And I will do
whatever you ask in my name, so that the Son may bring
glory to the Father. (John 14: 12-13)

If this is true of individual believers, as Jesus says, imagine what would be possible with corporate authority! Together, believers are able to fulfil the Lord's will and exercise authority over the enemy, over all these forces in rebellion to God. Disobedience in the Body of Christ can undermine the authority and powers among believers, and can give an opportunity to cause tension, friction and even division. It is difficult to exercise authority in such circumstances.

Finally, be strong in the Lord and in his mighty power.
Put on the full armour of God so that you can take your stand
against the devil's schemes. For our struggle is not against flesh
and blood, but against the rulers, against the authorities,
against the powers of this dark world and against the spiritual
forces of evil in the heavenly realms.
(Ephesians 6: 10-12)

Often there are victories to be won in spiritual warfare, in battles that are to be undertaken by a body of believers, rather than by isolated individuals, even though they are aware of the authority they possess as believers. Submitting to His authority is an indispensable and necessary function equipping the church congregation to overcome the evil powers and authorities in the unseen world.

The whole earth is under the power of the evil one and Christians need to be on the offensive, coming against those dark powers. This is the calling for the whole church. So whole congregations need to come to a position of submission, obedience and authority to be able to overcome and be triumphant. To allow disobedience and a lack of submission is going to weaken the authority of the whole congregation.

Therefore put on the full armour of God, so that when the day of evil comes, you may be able to stand your ground, and after you have done everything, to stand. (Ephesians 6:13)

When you consider how great God is, how can we even think of not obeying Him? Either personally or corporately?

The True Series will comprise the following titles:

TRUE ANOINTING
TRUE APOSTLES
TRUE AUTHORITY
TRUE CHURCH
TRUE COVENANT
TRUE DELIVERANCE
TRUE DEVOTION
TRUE DISCIPLES
TRUE FAITH
TRUE FREEDOM
TRUE GRACE
TRUE HEALING
TRUE HOLINESS
TRUE JUDGMENT
TRUE KINGDOM
TRUE LIFE
TRUE LORD
TRUE LOVE
TRUE MISSION
TRUE PRAYER
TRUE SALVATION
TRUE WISDOM
TRUE WORSHIP

All these books by Colin Urquhart and a catalogue of other titles and teaching materials can be obtained from:

Kingdom Faith Resources, Roffey Place, Old Crawley Road Faygate, Horsham, West Sussex RH12 4RU.
Telephone 01293 854 600 email: resources@kingdomfaith.com